"People of Orphalese, you can muffle the drum, and you can loosen the strings of the lyre, but who shall command the skylark not to sing?"

–Kahlil Gibran from his book "The Prophet"

Note for Librarians: A cataloguing record for this book is available from Library and Archives Canada at www.collectionscanada.ca/amicus/index-e.html
ISBN 1-4251-0214-x

Offices in Canada, USA, Ireland and UK

Book sales for North America and international:
Trafford Publishing, 6E–2333 Government St.,
Victoria, BC V8T 4P4 CANADA
phone 250 383 6864 (toll-free 1 888 232 4444)
fax 250 383 6804; email to orders@trafford.com
Book sales in Europe:
Trafford Publishing (UK) Limited, 9 Park End Street, 2nd Floor
Oxford, UK OX1 1HH UNITED KINGDOM
phone 44 (0)1865 722 113 (local rate 0845 230 9601)
facsimile 44 (0)1865 722 868; info.uk@trafford.com
Order online at:
trafford.com/06-1971

10 9 8 7 6 5 4 3

table of contents

Preface .7

iraq

War over...U.S. Troops come home! .11

How to exit .15

Subtle criticism .19

What to do .23

al-Zarqawi's death .27

Victims of conflict .31

terrorism

That growing pandemic .35

Capturing the leaders .37

leadership

Superpower status .41

Alarms going off .45

Loss of control .49

Great Britain .53

The Bush administration .57

Looking inward .61

The power in question 65
Eerie similarities 69

china

There is a looming dragon 73

big business

Lost our soul 77
On your own 81
Socialism 85

nuclear power

Political professionals 89

gas prices

Through the roof 93

nationalism

Age of nationalism 97

national disaster

Hurricane katrina 101

conservation

Global warming 105

the third world

Poverty and suffering 109

freedom

Democracy vs. freedom 113

warfare

The superpower 117
Nuclear capabilities 121

media

News coverage 125

government

Complex interplay 127
The threat 133
The Dubaiport 137
Out of control 141
The third party 145
Liberal or conservative 149
Social security system 153
Term limits 157

preface

A year of turbulence and a planet at unrest brings the year 2006 to a frustrating, yet challenging end. More questions than answers have been created.

As a spectator of the turbulence I have documented my observations on a weekly basis in a column which has been submitted to various newspapers throughout the country with one person's response to the ongoing crises of what I choose to call "the nature of things".

From the beginning of time there has been conflict of one kind or another and, for better or worse, that is the way it is. The complexity of human nature expresses itself in as many forms as there are individuals. It has been said by observers wiser than I that we do not resolve these ongoing problems, we merely manage them. Although each event is unique unto itself, at the same time they are merely reflections of similar events throughout history.

The method of crisis management and problem resolution is an ongoing process which allows us to grow and improve as a civilization. All of the angst which we encounter in the process is a part of the mechanism through which we are permitted to grow.

My critique of the many problems in 2006 hopefully has been submitted in a constructive format. I tend to be an optimist with a tinge of cynicism. I hope this is not anathema to those who choose to read the book. The views expressed are of a personal nature and hopefully will add to the national dialogue regarding our ongoing challenges.

iraq

War over...U.S. Troops come home!

That is the headline for which we are all waiting. The answer and solution to our problem in Iraq may not be simple, but it is staring us in the face.

The initial step must be taken by our leaders. All egos must be put on the table and the solution must be in the interest of the American people, in a war which is draining both our military and economic assets. We are precipitously approaching the "guns and butter" dilemma of the Johnson administration years earlier.

The configuration of the country of Iraq as we know it today has quite a short history. Formerly part of a larger entity called Mesopotamia, the current configuration was a result of a British decision after World War One; a decision arrived at by the British to facilitate their colonial goals at the time.

As was the case in Africa where countries were arbitrarily established not for the people of the area but for the foreign rulers at the time, the new configuration of Iraq cut across tribal and "natural" borders, thus creating the "artificial" borders of the area which we now call Iraq.

How do we reverse this series of mistaken series of decisions imposed upon the Iraqi people over the last century?

The theory that United States troops will assume a major presence in the country, until Iraqi troops are able to contain and control the insurgency within the country, is a flawed policy. The very presence of United States troops in the country is the most significant reason for not only the insurgency, but the support of many Iraqis against the "outside" occupiers. As mentioned earlier, we must put egos aside and make the major decision to withdraw our military forces from Iraq immediately to focus the problem from us to the people and "their" internal problem.

In terms of that problem, it would appear to me that there is a logical division within the current state the between Shiite, Kurdish and Sunni population. I would suggest that following the evacuation of United States and other foreign forces from the country, the Iraqi people themselves decide how the country is to be subdivided which will include not only the major entities within the country, but an equitable division of the natural resources of the country. That the process may not progress as "neatly" as a textbook does not matter. In the final analysis, it is they who must decide the future of the country.

iraq
How to exit

How do we exit from the uncomfortable corner into which we have apparently placed ourselves? That is the question for this writer in a less than popular war in Iraq. In fact, the answer is quite simple if you are a super power.

There are two options. First, if we see the war as winnable in a short and predictable time frame with minimal casualties this is the “good” scenario and we will have won the war on our terms, proven the international community incorrect in its evaluation of the war and guaranteed the upcoming election for the conservative forces in the country. On the other hand, if the outcome of the war is quite questionable, as many of us believe, the current administration must pursue quite a different strategy.

The first step in this alternative strategy of winning the war is to make full use of our dominant public relations position in the world. The planning behind this strategy is to actually refute all of our current strategy which is losing the war while at the same time suggest that we are pursuing the "other" strategy which some suggest will allow us a graceful exit from the war.

In other words black is white! Although this might seem somewhat devious and contradictory, it has in fact been done on many occasions by those in power. Words mean whatever you wish them to mean. This is the nature of diplomacy and international relations. If you are powerful enough, anything is possible.

The key to the decision making regarding the Iraq quagmire in which we find ourselves is to decide at what point in the conflict we make the critical decision to stay the war until we win on our terms or should this not be possible, to use an alternative exit strategy. Contrary to those who say we have no exit strategy, we do in fact have a strategy. The question is which of the two we use. On the one hand, if we are winning the war and project that the time frame for success is acceptable then we use plan one which is to manufacture the plan as we go which is in fact what we have been doing. If however we are not winning the war and there seems to be no realistic end in sight nor support by our allies, we then kick in plan number two. This brings into play our more creative strategy or what we shall call “the black is white strategy.” Keeping in mind that under this strategy we must exit the war at all costs since we see no viable end in sight, we “take over” all of those arguments of the opponents of the war and turn their arguments into ours by saying that we are actually doing what they are saying.

Sound confusing? Not actually, since we are using a strategy which has been employed throughout history. If you are powerful enough and losing an argument, you use your position of power to turn a weak strategy i.e., yours and turn it into a strong strategy i.e., theirs. So you see, in Iraq we cannot lose the war since we have created an exit strategy which fits all sizes.

iraq
Subtle criticism

If not now, when? The time for subtle criticism of the war in Iraq has passed. The war is essentially over and we have lost. All that remains is how we exit the area using whatever rationalizations are required. The strategy of how to terminate the war is no longer in our hands, it is in the hands of those Iraqis and their allies in the area whom we are opposing. It is they who will determine the outcome of the conflict. We are conducting essentially a defensive operation.

As loyal citizens it was our duty to support the initial decision to go to war after we were given the "facts" and logic to our involvement especially after the September Eleventh attack on our country. The President had cache with the citizens at that time. The issues for those of us who currently oppose the war were not apparent at that time. They are at this time quite clear.

First, the claim by the administration that Iraq had weapons of mass destruction and the danger to us was imminent turned out to be not true. Secondly, the current administration is attempting a connection between terrorism and Iraq. This is a specious argument to put it mildly and is an attempt to divide and conquer the administration's domestic audience. All but those few radicals in the country are opposed to terrorism and will do whatever it takes to defeat this enemy. The problem with the administration's attempt to connect terrorism with Iraq is that at the time, the American citizens were infuriated with the attack on our country and the President had to make some sort of concrete move against terrorism. Since the terrorists who are involved with this demonic movement were not located in a specific country or target at which we could retaliate, it was almost impossible for us to strike back. The administration had to take some specific action against terrorism or all hell would break out in this country, given the impatience of the citizenry. Iraq was the perfect faux enemy to choose, especially since Vice President Cheney was chomping at the bit to control the oil rich country of Iraq in addition to which President Bush needed little prompting from the vice president due to Iraq's shoddy treatment of his father. The scene was set for an elective war which we couldn't lose militarily. The problem was that military victory was but a small part of defeating the Iraqis

What has happened since our "military victory" is not only tragic, but not over yet by a long shot. Other allies cautioned us not to get involved in this "quagmire" without thinking of the potential ramifications. We were not in the mood to listen to anyone! In we plunged essentially on our own. The result has been catastrophic and continues today. From an economic point of view we have opened up a can of worms. We are essentially funding the war on our own and mortgaging the future by borrowing on the backs of our grandchildren. How long can we financially sustain such a debacle without the aid of international partners?

The question of casualties must be seriously examined. The fact is that over twentyfive hundred troops have died and the count goes on. Over seven thousand have been wounded and that count goes on. It is obvious that our high level of troop involvement is required just to maintain the status quo. If the international community is not willing to commit military assistance to this quagmire from where will the new troops be recruited? The unmentionable word "draft" must be considered. What will be the reaction of that vast Middle American population be if this draft be reinstituted? The Viet Nam demonstrations of thirty five years ago will be dwarfed by such an edict.

The vague, unsubstantiated and unrealistic connection between Iraq and terrorism must be broken and a new focus on one of the real source of terrorism and its causes must be centered on the Israeli –Palestinian conflict. Addressing that problem, a problem which has existed for over forty years in an even handed manner will begin the real solution to this seemingly unsolvable international problem.

The dilemma concerning the above scenario is that the higher the stakes, the more critical it becomes for the administration to not only defend its policy, but the more drastic steps it must take to justify such a flawed policy. The administration is quite aware of the repercussions which will be visited upon them by their own citizens should this flawed policy be elevated to the level of the Vietnam quagmire.

Well, here we are in 2006 and one of the burning questions remains. What do we do about our war in Iraq?

Those of us who opposed our invasion of Iraq from the beginning and those who have since changed their minds about the war are suggesting that the war is not winnable by outside interference; the war was a mistake from the first day and given this reality the Iraqis must solve their own problem. Our occupation as "caretakers" simply allows the Iraqi army NOT to take on their own responsibility and our armed forces are in fact giving the insurgents a foreign target upon which to not only vent their anger, but to mobilize elements of the Iraqi civilian population and upon which to focus their anger. We are accused by our brothers on the right of wanting to "cut and run" while those on the side of the administration suggest that should we "cut and run", we will be deserting our Iraqi brothers who have committed to a "free" and democratic Iraq. It is therefore our responsibility to ENSURE that there is a free Iraq.

My suggestion is that we have arrogantly assumed that WE can solve the future direction of Iraq when in fact our role allows us to merely participate in helping them make their own decision.

Both sides have hardened their positions and are unwilling to compromise these positions. I believe the administration is in a more vulnerable position since the American citizens will not tolerate a long drawn out war with mounting casualties and astronomically growing expenses with no short end in sight. Such an open ended war will only compromise and delay those urgent programs in our own country. It is revisiting the "guns and butter" argument of the Vietnam era.

The answer I suggest is rather simple and pragmatic. We are in complete control of the media and it is we who define in large part the "nature" of the war. The proper strategy and what I believe the administration is currently in fact creating, is to "construct" an exit strategy which will outline in detail how we exit Iraq AND ensure that the facts on the ground are reflecting the "paper" strategy. In short, what is actually occurring on the war front is not as important as what we SAY is happening. This gives us full flexibility to determine when we leave Iraq and on what terms. We have now accomplished our exit strategy.

Two final facts are in order. First, we will maintain a skeletal force inside and outside Iraq to guarantee our "position" for the future in the area and this force will be used tactically to keep the ground situation from getting out of control, although that may in fact not be possible but our tactical position will not expose us to the full commitment of our current dilemma. Second, should conditions, upon our withdrawal get out of hand and result in a civil war, we can claim that we left the country with a well trained Iraqi army and they failed to carry out THEIR responsibility.

This may appear a cynical and hypocritical solution to a problem which is currently central to our present unacceptable position in Iraq, but this is the reality of how domestic and international politics operate. If you have the power, you use it to maintain your control and outcome of a difficult position.

iraq
al-Zarqawi's death

For the last two days we have had wall to wall coverage of the killing of al-Zarqawi as though his death would be one more step in "turning the corner" in our war in Iraq.

Let us be quite clear. Al Zarqawi's removal from the scene in Iraq will have NOTHING to do with turning that corner. He is simply one of hundreds of leaders in the civil war in Iraq. Every time we eliminate one of the leaders in the movement against our occupation of the country, dozens of al-zarqawis types fill his shoes with that much more dedication to remove us from their country. His success and notoriety simply encourages other leaders who will fill his shoes in an effort to outdo that for which he has become famous.

The answer to the Iraq quagmire will come with two distinct occurrences.

1. Removal by whatever means necessary of ALL foreign interlopers.

2. Raising the standard of living of the poor and wretched people of Iraq. This will have to be done by whatever leadership eventually takes over the country. Should the process take a civil war so be it! As much as the current leadership in the United States would desire. The solution to that quagmire MUST come from within.

The word within truly means from within NOT puppet regimes put into power by the outside interlopers. Eliminate poverty and you will eliminate war!

Making such a huge media event of the elimination of al-Zarqari may give us that "good news" we so lack in that wretched war but that is all that we will receive. The war will go on and even intensify until we take the appropriate steps mentioned above.

iraq
Victims of conflict

We are all victims of this horrific conflict in Iraq. Through this administration's decision to go to war in Iraq based on false premises as was to be later revealed, we are all losers.

The Iraqi citizens, through no fault of their own have suffered multiple thousands of deaths and injuries as "bystanders" in the war. It has been said by the administration and its supporters that if we "cut and run" prematurely all hell will ensue if there is not a government in control of the country. Guess what? All hell is already breaking out in the country. The only difference is that it is on a longer and more insufferable pace which may go on for years whether or not we are present. For what it is worth, our very presence is one of the main reasons for the current carnage in the country.

The American military forces are the second victims in this "elective" war which the current administration has visited upon us. Our American youth have been put in a no win situation whereby they have been selected as that force to implement our current unenforceable policy. It is next to impossible for our military to identify enemy from friend and yet are forced to make on the spot decisions to kill or let live the Iraqis whom they encounter. The more this absurd policy continues the more enemies we will create among the Iraqi citizens. Being a "transparent" society, these missteps which may be taken by our soldiers through no fault of their own will come to light at which point we in the free and open society will be FORCED to prosecute our own soldiers. How impossible is this! We put our own soldiers in a no win decision making position and then we are forced to prosecute them. Is it any wonder that the American public is both confused and angry at such trials?

Finally it is the American citizen for whom this war is most tragic. As was the case with Vietnam, loyalties are broken down even among family members. The decision making leading up to our invasion of Iraq was not only poorly planned in terms of the big picture, but the policy was based upon misinformation and lies. Let the reader decide in his or her own mind if these decisions were made based upon ignorance or outright lies.

The miscalculation of our entry into Iraq has not been lost on those in the international community. Their lack of support is quite obvious and we have discovered belatedly that international support is quite necessary despite this administration's “go it alone” policy.” However, those in the international community are intelligent enough to separate the policy of this particular administration and the generous nature of America and its citizens. The sooner we terminate this fiasco in Iraq and bring in a new administration, the sooner we will again be viewed as the beacon of democracy; a goal to which all citizens of the world aspire.

terrorism

That growing pandemic

The size and cost of government is at the center of many discussions today. The expense of running government is gradually creeping at an exponential pace into our pockets.

One of the arguments put forth by many who are demanding a more responsible government is “term limits”. I would suggest that this would be like putting a band aid on a cancerous growth.

The term in office of our law makers is not at the core of solving our run away government. I would suggest that it is rather the benefits package given our elected leaders which is at the center of our problem with government.

In our personal budgets, it is we who control both our income and expenses. We are therefore quite aware when the balance between income and expense is getting out of control. The reason, obviously, is that it is OUR money about which we are talking. Unlike our personal budgets, the budget of the country which of course is OUR budget, writ large, is in the hands our elected officials. Herein exists the problem!

terrorism

Capturing the leaders

The headlines in one of the newspapers today read "Bin Laden's aide Abu Farraj al Libbi captured" We are led by administration sources to believe that we have captured a member of the upper echelon of the terrorist organization. As usual both politicians and military strategists are fighting this war with the same tactics used in previous wars.

The good news is that we have caught another terrorist leader. The bad news is that it doesn't matter! Prior to our invasion of Iraq, the terrorist structure and leadership chain was less complex than is the case today; at least that is what we are told. The invasions of Afghanistan and Iraq essentially fragmented the "organization" of the terrorist structure. It was, in effect, like turning the lights on in a kitchen which was infested with cockroaches. They all fled in various directions!

The point is quite simple. Those "name" terrorist leaders whom we are seeking are no longer the significant players in the game. The movement is now quite fragmented and to our disadvantage it is next to impossible to "cut the head off the beast"

Of course those name terrorist leaders whom we either capture or kill will give us great headlines, trophies and propaganda and that's about all. What we have created by flushing out our enemy terrorists is to allow them to create new and unnamed cells. The "stars" of these new movements will present themselves to us in various and creative confrontations in the future. In short, we have unsuccessfully confronted the terrorists and have created an open ended source for recruitment of new terrorists and new organizations.

What is needed to eliminate, or at least substantially reduce the plague of terrorism is a more creative approach to solving the problem. For starters we have to get Western interlopers out of the area thus eliminating a major source of irritation for those in the region, a solution to the Arab-Israeli problem by seriously acting as honest and objective brokers between the parties and finally a truly international effort by the more advanced countries of the world to alleviate poverty in the area. It is only then that we can begin the reconstruction in the area, both physical and psychological, and successfully confront this endemic movement.

leadership

Superpower status

Superpower status is accompanied by a corresponding superpower responsibility. There is no doubt that as of today the United States is by far the primary power in the world.

It is also true that no individual or nation is so powerful that corresponding responsibility is not inherited as part of wearing that crown. Outright arrogance, if not tempered with understanding and compassion towards others will result in a payback by those less powerful. The world is too large and complex for one superpower to rule without the assent and cooperation of some configuration of other nations surrounding that power. Superpowers come and go depending upon how they wear their crown.

Of course other less powerful nations will not directly challenge the preeminent superpower regardless of their deportment regarding the superpower's international strategy. What will ensue is a somewhat more devious and effective counter strategy. There is a natural inclination for those less powerful to envy those in power. A wise nation will use its power to solidify its base by disbursing some of its power to those lesser powers with whom they are involved. The benefit will be twofold. Firstly, by "sharing" power, at least minimally, your own strength and expansion of power will be enhanced. Second, and even more important, your superpower status will be less likely to be undermined by secretive alliances of lesser powers whose frustration is increasing due to your inappropriate and overbearing use of your power.

leadership
Alarms going off

When does the alarm go off? At what point do we connect the dots? Let me be quite clear. I have been against the Iraqi policy from the first day of the invasion. Having said that, in light of the devastation of New Orleans and the surrounding area by Hurricane Katrina, let us discuss the viability of conducting an open ended and, in these eyes, a non winnable and questionable war in Iraq while at the same time conducting an effective domestic program of homeland defense and the ability to respond to one or several national disasters.

As the super power of the world, some believe that we are capable of taking on ANY international challenge with or without allies. This is at best hubris in its most extreme form.

The Katrina event with its tragic and overwhelming results and our inadequate response, especially in the first few days, exposes our lack of priorities and systems in responding to events on the home front with our main focus on other areas of the world.

The capability of responding to an overwhelming crisis in one of our major population areas compounded by a sadly inadequate policy towards our border security problem should alert our leadership, once and for all that a “two front war” is folly, to put it politely, or devastating and self-destructive to put it in more blunt and straight forward terms.

Militarily, our under manned effort in Iraq has begun to burst at the seams. If we were to be successful in that war in Iraq, it would probably take three or four times the military force we now have employed and the war would STILL be open ended and the costs and commitment would be prohibitive. Our misuse of National Guard and Reserve forces has left us vulnerable at home and has disrupted thousands of families who had little expectation that the military person in the family would experience extended tours of duty outside the country.

The cost and time in repairing the overwhelming damage caused by the Katrina Hurricane will take billions of dollars and years of commitment. Even then we are not sure of the outcome in the area. In all probability, a permanent public works program will have to be set up, subsidized by the government, of course, to reconstruct the area. If the government is prudent, it should probably utilize those people whom the storm has directly affected to fill the thousands of positions required to address the disaster in and around New Orleans. And make no mistake; we are talking about a program which will have to be funded by the national government over many years.

This program, in addition to solidifying and expanding our sadly lacking homeland defense program will take all of our collective and national energies. We must start this superhuman effort by disconnecting ourselves from the fruitless and misdirected effort in Iraq. Whatever face saving rationale is used doesn't matter. The most realistic of which is to declare that we have given the Iraqi government the necessary tools to construct their own "democracy" and now it is time for them to take the burden of implementing their own form of democracy. The argument that "cut and run" is an unacceptable direction for the United States is, at best, faulty in its logic.

The Vietnam War and our departure should be proof enough. Almost forty years later the Vietnamese and their neighbors have solved their own problems, and our reputation has suffered little. I believe we sadly overestimate our role in the fortune or misfortune in the affairs of other nations. It is time that we, the superpower of the world mature and understand the proper and limited role for a superpower. Only then will we really comprehend the true nature and responsibility of such a lofty position.

leadership

Loss of control

Out of control! It can be no more delicately stated to make the point. In his first run for office, I sincerely wanted to see George W. Bush win the election. Although my politics lean towards the left, vice president Gore was, for me, quite unacceptable. His lack of personality and his bland and structured responses on issues were not only unappealing, but his patronizing personality was such that he appeared professorial in approach as though he were lecturing freshmen in a government 101 course. In short, he lacked the leadership qualities, in my mind, to be the next president of the United States.

George W. Bush, alternatively, seemed to be a "nice guy" who could draw on his father's associates to "bring him up to speed" in managing the country until he could establish himself as a true leader of the most powerful nation in the world. Not the best way to choose a president, but given the choices, in my mind, he was the better option.

His handling of the catastrophic attack in New York City was outstanding, and my choice seemed to be justified. Then a major crack in his armor appeared with the invasion of Iraq. Try as I might over the next year or so, I was unable to connect terrorism with the invasion of Iraq. I began looking at our president from a more critical and analytical perspective, beginning with his approach to restructuring Social Security, deepening deficit spending and taking control of national disasters such as Hurricane Kristina to mention the most obvious. He also displayed over this period of time, a rigidity and inability to compromise on any issue. Some might view this as a positive attribute to one's personality. For me, it indicated a lack of ability to look objectively at the other side of a given issue. That which also became obvious upon examining the policies of those decision makers surrounding the president was a hard line conservative agenda which either reflected the president's views or views to which he acceded of those conservatives surrounding him. This hard line conservative stance had the effect of dividing the nation rather than uniting the citizens in a common goal.

At this point, at least in these eyes, compromise with the "other side" was not acceptable despite the logic of any arguments challenging the conservative agenda.

The American people are most forgiving, especially towards their Commander in Chief. However, at a certain crucial point, the accumulation of questionable policies, at least to a large segment of the citizenry, such as those mentioned above, coalesce in the minds of the public. At that point a consensus of citizens may question its faith in leadership decision making. Their passions have now reached critical mass. They become active against a leader who will not, or at least chooses not to recognize the gravity and ramifications of his decision making.

It is indeed possible that we may hold our president to standards far above those of the ordinary citizen. That is the rightful nature of our expectations from the leader of the most powerful nation in the world.

The position of President of the United States is probably the most stressful circumstance to which one could be exposed. Those who aspire to this high position of trust and responsibility are aware, upon entering the office that this is part and parcel of the job and must accept the challenges of the position.

leadership
Great Britain

Shortly following the conclusion of World War II, Great Britain began her decline as one of the most powerful colonial powers on earth. The decline which had begun several years earlier accelerated precipitously upon the end of World War II.

Her rule over many countries of the world was glorious, at least in her eyes, and ceding this power must have been an extremely painful process, as tends to be the case with those in positions of power. To her credit, Great Britain has always, and continues today to have a unique "style" which most nations not only recognize, but possibly consciously or subconsciously try to emulate. As an anti Colonialist, I did not approve of her period of domination; however, even during the extended period of colonialism, save periods of a less than enlightened guardianship, her "style" was ever present.

Having said that, her acceptance and transition to her new role as a second level power in the world was not voluntarily accepted; rather it was thrust upon her as a result of a changing world power structure led by the United States and not far behind, the Soviet Union.

Today, there is a similar process occurring. The United States, the most powerful nation on earth since approximately 1945 is currently being challenged by powers in the Far East, namely China and India. The emergence of these two massive powers is well upon us. Some say that they will not reach their zenith, if at all, for several decades. This may or may not be true but given the exponential expansion of information and technology through the internet and the brain power being developed in those areas, there is a new time frame in terms of change throughout the world. That change may be upon us more quickly than many expect. It is suggested by some that by the mid twenty first century there will be a sea change in power relations among nations and the power locus may indeed shift from the West to the East.

As was the case with Great Britain, it is hoped that if this sea change does in fact occur, the United States will accept the change with the dignity and grace with which Great Britain accepted her new international role in an ever changing world environment.

leadership

The Bush administration

It is time for us to put the current Bush administration behind us. The title of "world leader" for better or worse is placed in the hands of that country which is the leader not only militarily, but spiritually and in terms of a world view which reflects the aspirations and dreams of the world community in general.

This administration has lost sight of that world view. We currently have a world view which rules by fear and intimidation. I would surmise that any opinion poll reflecting the general population of the world would reflect anger and fear of this current administration.

When the first feedback of our invasion of Iraq was measured, by an overwhelming majority of the “people” of the world, the strategy and rationale of the invasion of Iraq was rebuffed. I remember clearly at that time, and I will willingly admit that we were still staggering from the attack on our country by terrorists, the feeling by MANY Americans, including our leadership was that we were right as regards our invasion strategy of Iraq and to hell with world opinion. Since that time, we have learned that most, if not all of the rationale for invasion Iraq was based on false premises. Whether it was ignorance and misinterpretation on the part of the administration or we were PURPOSELY misdirected by our leaders will have to be determined by historians sometime in the future. Regardless, we have been at war with Iraq for over four years and the negative opinion regarding world renunciation of our invasion by the Bush administration has softened, not because the administration has changed its view, but because of the fact that we have failed to prove our case not only on the ground, but in terms of swaying the opinion of those who opposed the invasion and its implications.

There was a time, and not that long ago, when our leadership was respected throughout the world save those who would never support us regardless of the cause. Today, those who support our cause not only in Iraq, but regarding our world view in general are represented by very few world leaders save those "client" governments who are in support of our current direction.

America and its goals and aspirations have always been the envy of worldwide opinion and to live in a country other than the United States would be unacceptable, at least to this writer. What we must DEMAND from the next administration is restoration of our position as world leader in terms of progressive ideas which reflect the dreams and aspirations of people of the world INCLUDING those of us in the United States who still believe in these ideals.

The world community must be convinced again that we are a great people in a great nation which espouses those ideas of freedom and democracy which have been representative of our country in the past. Above all, they must be convinced that THIS administration does NOT represent that dream which people throughout the world including American citizens have long aspired.

leadership
Looking inward

The time has come for us to look inward to evaluate our current position as the world super power since we have occupied this lofty position for over fifty years.

Just as in our personal lives we must face the fact that our lives are finite and we must accept death as a phase in our lives, so we must as a nation face the fact that the designation as "world superpower" is also but a passing phase in the larger history of the world. The time and place when the throne must be handed to the next contender or wrested from the current "occupant" may not be evident at the time of the change, but there are certain indicators which one can observe to serve as "warning signals" that change is coming.

As regards the current resident of this lofty position as world leader, I would suggest that there are two, and maybe more, quite clear indicators that the change is not only imminent, but may already be in play. It will usher in a dramatic change in power relations among the current nations of the world. The change at the top will reverberate from the very strongest of nations to the smallest and most insignificant nations of the world.

The first indicator of the sea change which may well be upon us is a general unease by many nations of the world in their perception of the current world leader as a benchmark and model from which they can emulate and duplicate as that ideal to which they can aspire.

The current administration under George W. Bush has taken that model which has been envied and admired by most nations of the world and turned it into a symbol which is no longer that model to which most nations aspire. The very time of this change in attitude is quite precise. Our invasion of the country of Iraq, a strategic decision which was challenged by many nations of the world was that point at which world opinion of our country was seriously questioned. Let us be quite clear that world opinion of the United States is not directed at either the American people or their way of life, it is specifically directed at the current leadership of the country.

Unfortunately, it is not possible to separate the people of the United States from that current leadership which is directing current policy. The point is that the role of world leader is defined not only by our power position in the world, but by those ideas which represent to the world that ideal towards which all countries of the world can aspire. We have currently lost sight of that ideal!

That lofty position of world leader is difficult to maintain and one must take constant vigilance to preserve that coveted position.

Current world affairs play a key role in determining whether or not the existing world power retains its position. When a vacuum occurs regarding the legitimacy of world leadership by a given nation that vacuum will be filled by the next in line.

Today that role of world leader is being challenged from the East. Specifically, China, Russia and India together and separately are challenging the primacy of The United States as world leader. How long this process will take to play out if and when it is to be successful is still to be determined. One ominous sign is the current role of China in South America.

This is indeed ominous for those of us in North America. The United States must recreate its image in the area. The fact is that many people in South America do not trust the current administration in the United States and it is a fact that some of the key leaders in the area are looking elsewhere for leadership and are finding a well funded and militarily growing ally in China. They DO have a viable and realistic option! The confluence of events in history seems to be lining up for a sea change in world power relations.

From a personal point of view, I am not quite ready for the United States to cede world leadership. We must therefore do our part in generating new leaders in the country who truly represents and recaptures that idealism worthy of world leadership.

leadership

The power in question

Sliding from the position of the most powerful nation in the world to either second rate world power or more realistically a position of sharing world power status can be quite painful. During this process the power in question continues to "act" like the most powerful nation in the world while in fact the leverage begins to erode and "other" nations begin to display subtle and in some cases not so subtle displays of power. Legends do not die easily and the "role" of world leader slowly erodes and is diffused to the point when finally recognition of the fact becomes obvious.

One of the symbols of world leadership is the United Nations structure in New York City. As the United States, the current world leader begins to dismiss some of the authority of the world body the process is already in progress. The building itself is additionally in massive disrepair and renovating and updating the structure would cost many millions of dollars.

It would perhaps be possible to see the vision of a NEW United Nations building constructed in another country. In fact that structure might be located in China. This is not such a far fetched theory and should this monumental change take place the "changing of the guard" might be the first step in a realignment of power between nations of the world. Paraphrasing a philosopher of yore, "the only thing that is permanent is change."

leadership

Eerie similarities

There is an eerie similarity to that which is occurring to the Palestinian people under Hamas rule and that which occurred under Saddam Hussein in Iraq years ago. At that time, due to the fact that the ordinary citizens were being punished unjustly because of sanctions by the international community against Saddam Hussein the outside powers finally had to relent and limit aid to the Iraqi people to non strategic aid. Of course Saddam used this opening in the sanctions to his advantage.

There is a movement today to bypass the Hamas rulers to funnel international aid directly into the pockets of the citizens under Hamas rule. I suspect there will be a similar outcome to this benevolent program aimed at relieving the suffering of the common Palestinian people.

This having been said, I believe there is no other option. Should we continue our current sanctions against the government it will use this hardship upon the people as a tool to incite the citizens against the outside forces claiming that it is these very outside forces which are in fact causing the hardships being inflicted upon them.

An unstable and angry population is the last scenario needed in an area which is already simmering with discontent and massive unemployment and poverty. The policy of some current international forces trying to "starve" the Hamas leadership into submission to THEIR agenda is succeeding only in feeding this hatred of outside influences. In the final analysis it is to their own leadership they will turn for support, not to outside anti Hamas factions.

What is required by these anti Hamas international forces is to disregard the Hamas rhetoric which is in fact a defense mechanism to protect the collective egos of the leadership. In place of this misplaced strategy what must emerge is a POSITIVE strategy to reinforce a popular leadership and guide it into a direction of peace and growth in the area which will play a large part in the major problem in the area which is unemployment and poverty.

china

There is a looming dragon

There is a looming dragon out there. The "Sleeping Dragon" has been awakened! Back in the 1950's when China was asleep and an object of scorn by other powers she was being tutored by Russia in terms of establishing her identity as a Communist state.

Even at that time it was instructive to note that China, despite her weakness, would not take the path suggested by her Russian ally. She would instead decide to follow her own instincts and began the Great Leap Forward on her own.

Some suggest that the price for her rise to the status of world power was too harsh on its citizens. One must remember that China, at that time, had an overwhelming population of peasants with a peasant mentality. That mentality had to be "broken" to thrust the nation into the current century. The forced regimentation of its citizens with the accompanying sacrifices has resulted in her status of a world power today.

It is this writer's prediction that the second half of this century will belong to China. By the end of the century it will be one of the preeminent world powers. This observation is offered for several reasons. First, the very size of the country which consists of a full twenty five percent of the world population must be considered. The numbers alone give it a decided edge. Second, the Chinese people have always been an industrious population. In an industrial age, this must be considered an asset. Thirdly, the focus of the family has always been education and an educated and intelligent population is a force which must be taken seriously. Lastly, the nation has found the magic key of industrialization. Their record of industrial growth in the last twenty years has been nothing short of a miracle.

The one caveat which this writer must offer is that China's use of raw materials has, and will continue to pressure world wide resources. This is a potentially serious problem which it is hoped the leadership in the country is aware and has the foresight and circumspection to see the "big picture" and assumes a responsible structured growth.

big business
Lost our soul

Where did we lose our soul? It was not that long ago when there was a symbiotic relationship between employer and employee. Granted both parties had their own self enlightenment as part of that which they brought to the bargaining table.

Of course employees have always had as a primary motive for their employment support of their family and personal growth. The corporation for its part was always focused on profitability but not at the expense of their employees, at least within the reasonable profit structure of the corporation. These positions were not contradictory. In fact, long term employment of their employees was looked upon in a very positive light by the corporation. Longevity was tied directly into reliability, stability and profitability due in part to low turnover rate and all that entailed.

Correspondingly, the employees could depend upon a long term "contract" which would allow them safe haven for both their family and personal growth and a longer vision of a safe retirement. Key to this arrangement was predictability for both parties.

During the last decade or so, words like longevity reliability and safe haven have disappeared from the lexicon of both parties, especially from the point of view of the employer. The symbiotic relationship has evolved into a state of survival of the fittest.

The bottom line profitability each quarter has become quite pervasive to corporate strategy. In addition, cheap overseas labor has become part of this equation. It can be argued that we have to keep a competitive edge by exporting jobs and of course there is some truth to this mantra.

Longer term considerations however must be factored in as part of the changing relationship between employer and employee. One important element of the current growing dysfunction in the workplace is employee attitude. Pride in product or service being rendered has long been a centerpiece of the American workplace. With the changing attitude of the employer towards his employee is it any wonder that pride in workmanship has diminished? With lack of security and longevity of his employment can we expect the employee to feel that he is part of a team?

In the short term, the corporation will "make its quarterly bottom line" but we should be more concerned with the longer term deterioration of not only the product and service we offer, but a possible chaotic and survival of the fittest attitude where each individual is concerned only with his personal short term goals. I suggest that this is about as close as one can come to a recipe for disaster and a guarantee of a decline in the nation as a superpower.

big business
On your own

You're on your own! That is the clear message. It is like the perfect storm where all of those elements come together to form that condition which results in a sea change in the relationship between government and the governed.

It seems that almost overnight many of the existing relations between the citizens and their government have been changed.

Job security and longevity have disappeared due to the global economy.

Company pensions are becoming dinosaurs and are being replaced with 401K type employee funded retirement plans thus relieving the responsibility of traditional retirement programs from the company and placing them squarely upon the shoulders of the employee.

Health insurance has increased astronomically, and that benefit formerly paid by the employer now has become the basic responsibility of the employee.

As is the case with the perfect storm, there may be disastrous consequences just around the corner. The fact that responsibility for survival has been placed squarely on the shoulders of the citizens might have the following consequences.

Loyalty to the company may become outdated in the blink of an eye since the very reasons for that loyalty will no longer be present.

If that "family" atmosphere at the workplace which has been the hallmark of our nation for these many years which of course involves a self—interest on the part of both employees and employers disappears, the resulting potential anarchy and self preservation in the workplace may ensue leading directly to weakening of the very structure of our free enterprise system.

This potentially apocalyptic and yes, somewhat cynical view of the current state of affairs in the nation needs to be addressed as the crisis which it is or the apocalypse to which I refer may in fact become reality.

big business
Socialism

In a recent article I suggested that the age of nationalism was coming to a creeping yet imminent conclusion due to the globalization of communications and the emergence of a new way of conducting business. "Workers of the world unite!" was the cry earlier in the twentieth century of the Socialist Movement. Socialism remains today, albeit a shadow of its earlier manifestation.

The labor movement is in danger of self-destructing due to the internal turmoil and fracturing of the movement. From within there is dissention and the competing groups are struggling for leadership in the movement. The old guard is calling for the movement to unite to battle the current dominance of the Republican Party and the anti-labor movement prevalent throughout the country. The new faction within the labor movement is calling for drastic change and is challenging the old way of doing business.

It would appear that both sides are firmly entrenched in their positions and as both sides harden their stance, the labor movement becomes less and less effective against an opponent, i.e., the forces of big business which are currently dominating the business environment.

Big business has been first to identify and respond to the new "world order" of business on an international basis. Still behind the curve is organized labor. To this day its call is for a united stance against big business in the United States, though the leadership is split on exactly how to combat the current forces of the organized forces of corporate America.

Notwithstanding the fact that "internationalism" of big business is not yet formalized, the dominant large businesses in the United States understand that the future lies in being part of the internationalism of business, yet the labor movement has yet to accept the reality. To combat an international opponent i.e., big business on equal grounds, labor must also unite on an international basis. Until this reality becomes apparent to the labor movement in this country the union movement will continue to decline and face an incremental growth by big business which will continue to dominate and control the "rules and regulations" of how business is done, unfortunately at the expense of "organized" labor. It is incumbent upon some leader in the labor movement to stand up and even the playing field.

nuclear power
Political professionals

Most of the political professionals are falling in line with the administration's view that we have to stop North Korea and Iran from developing a nuclear power base.

The logic is that if these "evil" empires develop nuclear capabilities they will not only obviate peace in their area of influence but could precipitate war with their neighbors and eventually spread to other areas of the world. I tend to be somewhat cynical in my views. I maintain that all politicians should be viewed with quite a bit of skepticism.

Let me suggest that there is another agenda to which we are not privy. China is a prime example of a once "evil" empire and even today it is still considered by some evil. China acquired the status of nuclear power quite a few years ago. Wait a minute! Why hasn't China used its leverage to take over the rest of Asia? Part of the answer is quite simple.

Along with the prestige of becoming a nuclear power is the obligation of not using it as a weapon. Its power is in the "threat" of using the weapons not actually using it. You see, if you are sophisticated enough to develop nuclear weapons, you are also intelligent enough to understand that should you use the weapon, other "enemies" might use it on you. In fact by using the weapon you will probably guarantee your own destruction. In other words, the result is a lose/lose situation.

We now come to the essence of why we don't want North Korea and Iran to develop a nuclear capability. Our disdain for these "evil" nations and their attempts at acquisition of such nuclear weapons lies in the fact that should they acquire their own independent nuclear capability they will have developed "leverage" thus giving them a sort of parity with us. We who are in the nuclear family enjoy our privileged position and will not allow these outside evil empires to join the club.

It is like the magician who dazzles you with his feats using his right hand strategically to befuddle you while pulling the "scam" with his left hand. Likewise, we hide our real agenda i.e., not sharing power with those whom we consider enemies and emphasize that portion of the argument which stipulates that if these "enemies" acquire nuclear capabilities war will be imminent.

The fact is that if these "enemies" acquire nuclear capabilities they will be quite reluctant to use them understanding that retaliation will be immediate and devastating. On the other hand, these "evil" empires clearly understand that by acquiring nuclear power status they will acquire the leverage they currently lack and insure that the "free" nations who have nuclear capabilities will hesitate to confront them thus equalizing the equation.

I never cease to be amazed at the two levels at which all governments operate. On the one hand we in the public are given that which will support their argument. On the other hand the "real" agenda is forever hidden. This "game" is played by all nations.

gas prices
Through the roof

Gas prices are going through the roof! The response of the American people appears to be like that of lemmings, falling in line and leaping from the cliff with neither rhyme nor reason, or so at least it appears to this observer. A cynical writer, years ago, indicated that the American people were like a nation of sheep following one another almost automatically without logically challenging their leaders on given critical issues, and with neither the resolve nor ability to question and take action on those decisions being made by their own government.

Gas prices have been ratcheted up penny by penny over the past year until they have reached not only astronomical levels, but have become unreasonably and unacceptably burdensome on the average American citizen, and it is to those citizens of whom I speak. Other citizens who are fortunate enough to exist above the level of existence on their paychecks have the ability to "factor in" these huge gas increases into their budget and are thus unwilling to "rock the boat".

There are those however, and I speak of the millions of citizens who live from paycheck to paycheck and who do not have the "flexibility" to adjust their budgets without cutting into other critical aspects of their lifestyles and which may adversely affect their level of existence. For purposes of space, I will mention only briefly that it is not only the price at the gas pump which is at issue, but the thousands of businesses which must adjust their prices due to the high cost of oil thus adding to the burden of that increasing number of suffering American citizens.

What then can be done for these unfortunate citizens whose lives and futures are in the hands of what appears to be an unthinking and uncaring leadership both in the private and public sectors?

What is most interesting about our politician class of citizens is that when easy decisions are required, it is they who take "responsibility". On the other hand when hard decisions are to be made, they indicate that "we" must make hard choices. In other words, the responsibility is "ours" not "theirs".

The United States is the most powerful country in the world. The reason given for the high price of gas is that the international demand is outstripping the ability of the oil produces to meet this demand. That is the "cookie cutter" answer to the current high prices at the gas pumps. And that is only the beginning of the dilemma. It appears that prices will continue to rise, at least for the foreseeable future.

What then is the answer to the quandary in which we find ourselves? I suggest that we the people tell our government, in no uncertain terms, that gas prices have to be both brought down to reasonable prices and kept there! How they perform this "miracle" in light of the international growing demands for oil is THEIR problem, not ours. Our government must realign it's priorities to accommodate this "adjustment". It will probably require taking money out of one pocket and putting it into another, as we all do during times of crisis. We must force them to take some money out of their pocket i.e., their own protected priorities and putting it into ours. It is about time we ALL feel the pain equally. Only when THEY feel the pain on a personal level will change occur.

nationalism

Age of nationalism

The age of nationalism may be quickly coming to an abrupt and natural death. Methods of communications have become internationalized and with the speed and freedom of these new forms of communications, nationalism may be dying a death similar to that of the horse and buggy with the advent of the automobile. People and nations of similar interests speak to each other beyond national borders and their "allegiance" is to others who may not even be in the same hemisphere. The concept is not revolutionary, in fact such observers as Thomas L. Friedman in his new book "The World is Flat" is one of the leading exponents of this new phenomenon.

Prominent governmental and business leaders have already come to this conclusion and are trying to “ease” the American public into the new reality. One of the problems in this “flattening of the globe” is the fact that those who are currently “managing” the world and who enjoy a rather exclusive hold on those benefits of being the subject rather than the object of the current international situation may not choose to cede their position of primacy to a world community in which they have held the privileged position. Ceding this role of preeminence is not just an academic exercise.

Witness our current situation in the United States. The relationship between the rich and poor, and indeed the relationship between United States citizens and foreign less fortunate citizens is one in which we in the “have” position may sympathize with the deplorable conditions of others who are less fortunate, but to give more than lip service or sympathy which takes “nothing out of our pockets” is about the extent to which we are willing to contribute.

Leveling the “playing field” will take not only a superhuman effort by those of us in the “have” nations, but will take sacrifices which will surely affect our current lifestyles. Blaming rising third world powers such as China and India for the current quandary in which we find ourselves may be good fodder for the politicians who as usual want to “cover their tails” but will not suffice in this era of sea change.

Our true statesmen, if there are any such animals available, will have the daunting and courageous task of informing and educating the American public of the rapidly changing relations between nations and the sacrifices which must be made to facilitate a peaceful process which is becoming as inevitable as night following day.

national disaster
Hurricane katrina

Hurricane Katrina, that devastating storm of this new century is an incident which will be etched in our collective memories for the rest of our lives. The media will have hours of commentary on the subject, books will be written and thousands of words will have been spewed out examining and critiquing this "once in a lifetime" phenomenon and not unexpectedly, a TV movie will doubtless ensue in short order.

I will choose therefore not to add my commentary to the excessive coverage of the event other than to mention that almost all will agree that the response was overly delayed and ineffective and that the obligatory "blame" will be spread evenly from individuals who could, but chose not to leave, to local officials who failed to act in a more timely manner and to our president who has the ultimate power AND responsibility to demonstrate leadership in such times of crisis. Repercussions for this lack of leadership will most certainly plague the nation for years to come.

I choose rather to take a short introspective examination as I write this article from a more secure and comfortable perspective overlooking the bay in Quincy. That separation between me and those thousands of victims in and around New Orleans is but a matter of chance.

As we journey through life, we surround ourselves with family, friends, acquaintances and "things" which define who we are. As the astronauts looked down from the darkness of outer space, they and we, through our televisions could dramatically observe the fragile and beautiful object that our planet presented from such a unique perspective.

At that time, and more importantly at the present, the uniqueness and fragility of our existence becomes dramatically obvious. The reality of that world which we have constructed around ourselves is but a thin and delicate veneer which at any moment could be terminated and our lives could be permanently changed and possibly destructed in the blink of an eye. The veracity of that superficial and delicate veneer has been suddenly brought to my attention and all of those assumptions around which I have structured my existence on this beautiful planet have been put in a more realistic and even alarming perspective.

conservation

Global warming

Global warming is here! Have we finally gotten the message? The international community has been sending us signals for years. We have, to date, been rejecting the message. This reluctance to directly confront the problem is in all probability based largely upon the enormous costs involved in implementing programs to confront this global crisis and its effect on the nature and scope of the way we prioritize our way of doing business and the possibly disorienting effect on the business community which has to date been unable to factor in global warming into its equation of the cost of doing business.

Well, Kristina, the current hurricane affecting the New Orleans and Biloxi areas hopefully has brought the message home once and for all. It will be noted that the water temperature near the surface south of New Orleans was over 90 degrees! This high water temperature is the fuel which feeds the hurricanes and intensifies its core thus increasing the ferocity of the storms with the accompanying extremely high tides and devastation to the land area when the hurricane strikes.

Costs of these increasingly ferocious storms go directly to the pocketbooks of the American people. This message should not only go directly to the American people, but to the leadership in the country. The costs and devastation of these increasingly ferocious hurricanes visiting us will increase exponentially and will force us to directly confront the growing problem of global warming.

The connection between the fuel, i.e., warmer waters and the increasing intensity and destruction must be obvious. The cost of responding to these increasingly intense hurricanes is increasing at a frightening pace. One does not have to be a rocket scientist to see that the cost out of our pockets is now rising to an unacceptable level.

It is time for our politicians, most of whom are not blessed with courage, to step forward and inform the leadership in the country that global warming must be dealt with NOW. We have no other option short of destruction of the planet for the penalty of inaction to this global threat is both dire and irreversible.

the third world

Poverty and suffering

The acute and unacceptable level of poverty and suffering present in many third world countries is a well documented fact and is verified by the many studies by well intentioned international Millennium type study groups held in exotic locations such as Reykjavik, Iceland.

These study groups, in much detail, focus on general areas such as poverty, AIDS, women's rights, the high death rate of young children, the individual economies of third world countries with their peculiarities, political leadership, corruption in government and other such important issues.

At such meetings, the problems are undoubtedly discussed in depth with thousands of documents produced as evidence going into the meetings, and a similar number of documents generated as a result of the meetings with the obligatory critiques of the current situation with grand programs offered to alleviate the problem.

My concern with the current approach to resolution of this international crisis is that the solutions, as enlightened and well meaning as they may be, are lofty and idealistic programs which although well directed, are unrealistic in terms of achievability.

My proposed approach to structuring an agenda with a more realistic prospect of implementing a program with achievable and measurable results would be the following:

Continue the current approach which, if nothing else, will reemphasize the urgency of the current situation while implementing a more realistic program set forth in my next point.

Select one country, preferably small and with relative stability which would permit those of us in the international community to use in a pilot case study into which we should put all of our collective energies to COMPLETELY structure and manage including whatever financing is required for this INVESTMENT. This will permit us to observe first hand our investment, the problems involved and our hands on management of a third world country. If we are to implement this program, we must assume complete authority, as paternalistic as this might appear, to structure a functioning prototype for this test third world country. We would at this point have an ideal working model and at the appropriate time, control of this new entity would be turned over to the leaders of the newly formed nation.

The above approach, if properly implemented might well be the beginning of the end of poverty and deprivation in the third world thus allowing the new nations to contribute both economically and politically to the world community. A caveat should be inserted at this point given my skeptical and at times cynical nature of world politics. If, and I hope this is not the case, The United Nations, and I include all of those members of this august body, in addition to doing good for the world might have the personal priority of maintaining their positions through continuation of this world problem. This would of course result in a major impediment to solving this third world crisis. They need not worry. For if they have the foresight and enlightenment they will realize that once this problem has been successfully resolved, other and ongoing crises will replace the current crisis thus allowing the United Nations to continue its productive role as world problem solver. The time has arrived where we must stop giving the third world countries fish to eat and to teach them how to fish!

freedom

Democracy vs. freedom

It must be said here that there may well be a substantive difference between democracy and freedom. Our current policy in the war in Iraq, at least from this person's perspective, has been to create a Western style democratic form of government in the "new" Iraq. I would submit that our first error in judgment is that we are making an attempt to create "our" democracy in a country which has minimal, if any experience with our form of Western Democracy. In fact, it appears that the upcoming election in October may be "tainted" in that the Shiite majority (with the assent or maybe even persuasion of the United States) is "restructuring" the election to almost ensure the positive outcome of the process.

I would further suggest that there is an "arrogance of power" in our assertion that ALL Iraqis should live in a democratic state as is the case in the United States of America.

My suspicion is that most Iraqis, although probably aspiring to freedom in their lives, have a definition of democracy which might well differ substantially from our definition of that same concept.

It may well be impossible for the United States, superpower of the world, to envision a “different” type of democracy and therein may lie part of the problem in our current strategy in Iraq. We are, in my opinion, going down the wrong road with our current occupation of the country. Our rigid approach in the current strategy does not permit us to “connect” with the citizens of Iraq. It may indeed be that NO successful outside strategy is possible in that battered nation. The fact that we got rid of an evil dictator was good in and by itself although invasion of the country seemed, again in these eyes, quite a bit of overkill and has put us in a position, the extrication from which may well be impossible without some face saving strategy.

Democracy is a concept which has an individual definition for each participating nation. This may be even more substantive in a nation which has no formal history of a western style democracy.

The route to democracy in Iraq, if it is to be, will probably necessitate a quite different journey from that envisioned by those of us in the United States. It may in fact involve a civil war, to which we may be unwitting partners, to sort out the players and the end result, if successful, may be a form of government unrecognizable from that "traditional" form of that which we call democracy. So be it! Let the process play out on THEIR terms. It is THEIR dream.

warfare
The superpower

Superpower advanced technology warfare pitted against an enemy with low technology defense from the third world on their territory. What we have here is an interesting struggle being played out on the battlefield. At first glance, the battle seems quite unequal and the results should be quite predictable. Let us look at the "assets" and "liabilities" of both sides and hopefully put the battle into a clearer perspective.

The superpower has an ideal "testing ground" to experiment with the latest weaponry and advanced military tactics in a "real time" situation where its military tactics and strategy are given full freedom to experiment with its new "toys".

There is no doubt that the superpower with its advanced technology could easily defeat a rag tag army of the third world country in short order. We need go no further than the latest invasion of Iraq. At this point, the argument becomes more interesting. We now move into phase two of the war. Once the invasion is complete and the advanced superpower has occupied the territory there is a noteworthy change in the power relationship. Now that the invader has occupied the land it must (1) protect itself (2) eliminate the enemy and (3) win over the minds and hearts of the people. This is easier said than done for two reasons. First, it must separate the enemy forces from its own citizens which becomes complicated due to the fact that since the enemy has retreated back into the rest of the population, it thus makes it difficult to identify that very enemy and in an attempt to eliminate the enemy, civilian casualties are necessarily involved thus alienating portions of the very people they are trying to "liberate". Next, unless the war is ended in short order, it becomes open ended which has unexpected, or maybe not so unexpected ramifications. The people at home, accustomed to quick and decisive solutions to most problems, as is the case in most advanced societies, become restless because of the "open ended" nature of the engagement.

With this kind of commitment two inevitabilities surface (1) the war becomes costly with possibly no end in sight and (2) casualties begin to mount. Under this scenario time becomes the enemy of the superpower.

On the other side, the "rag tag" third world forces have now altered the chess game in their favor. Prior to the invasion, there was no way, given their technology, which they could effectively retaliate against the superpower. Now that the enemy has put himself in their territory and they can now 'have at him". The timeframe of the war does not matter to him. He is fighting for his country and the acceptable timeframe or method of retaliation has no boundaries.

One of the most effective methods to counter the occupation is sabotage on an ad hoc basis so the invading forces can never tell where or when the insurgents may strike. A second and even more insidious form of guerrilla warfare is the adaptive method of such warfare. In the beginning, the invading forces wreak heavy casualties upon the insurgents, but the insurgents are quite adaptive and not only do they develop methods to minimize their casualties, but they create newer and more devastating methods to attack their superior and better equipped invaders.

I would suggest that given the unpredictable nature of war between nations, it would behoove any nation, large or small to evaluate thoroughly the precipitation of such an event and ensure that it have international backing prior to commitment to such an event. The stakes, especially in modern times are too high and the outcome too unpredictable.

warfare
Nuclear capabilities

If it were not for the Iraq war in our rear view mirror, I would have said in response to the "rumor" of a possible tactical nuclear attack on Iran that a planted story from the "left wing Bush haters" was a possibility. At this point and with hindsight of the Iraq fiasco I take the "rumor" very seriously. Bush and his right wing advocates seem to have a messianic mission to save the world for democracy.

Certain proponents of the strategy to deprive Iran from acquiring nuclear capabilities will stop at nothing including all out war to prevent this eventuality. These proponents suggest that tactical nuclear precision bombing will deprive the Iranians from acquiring this nuclear capability. It seems incredulous to me, in light of our Iraqi experience, that should we take such a momentous step which is in fact declaring war on Iran, that they will not take the obvious measures to protect their country. This will of course include drawing us into a land war. This is precisely the poor planning we encountered in our Iraqi adventure.

We will have opened the proverbial can of worms. It will be at their discretion as to the methods and locations which will be their targets. Again, we will probably have committed the same error which has us tied down in the Iraqi quagmire. High technology and superior firepower can afford us the initial advantage. This initial advantage however has its limitations. The world is now a complex and intertwined stage and unless all of the pieces fall into place, no one power, regardless of its primacy can wage a successful military adventure on its own.

The current tension between the United States and Iran is an example which should be carefully analyzed from many angles before commitment to such a campaign.

The first and obvious element in such analysis is the factor of oil. Iran has vast quantities of this strategic asset and should such a conflict arise between the two powers, not only the flow of oil, but the potential astronomical cost per barrel must be taken into consideration and its effect on the world community.

Second, the impact on the current war in Iraq must be considered. Iran with its enormous Shiite population could wreak havoc on our military position in Iraq. The type of warfare if such an eventuality were to occur will not be on our terms. The warfare will not be the classic historical type of war which fills our military tomes on strategic warfare.

Disruption of the flow of oil through the Persian Gulf would be another potential disastrous element that would be added to the already complex equation.

Finally, other powers in the area have complex and growing relations with Iran, namely Russia and China to mention the major players in the scenario. The United States alone cannot expect unilaterally to wage a successful war in the area and cooperation of the world community, or at least those countries in the area seems next to impossible.

My opinion is that there are certain countries in the world which are "destined" to be major players on the world scene based on size of the country, strategic location, resources and most importantly being in a place in history when it is their turn to be one of the superpowers in the world. Whether or not Iran fits this measurement of a potential superpower will have to be played out. Should they in fact fit this mould, they will find out as have we that the position of superpower comes with certain obligations and potential liabilities. They will encounter these positive and negative aspects of power should they be fortunate enough to rise to their expectations.

Our role in the changing nature of the balance of power in the world will play out as it has in the past and we will either be able to accommodate a new player in the international arena or challenge its legitimacy. The result will be whatever it is and our fate will be determined either by the accommodation or challenge to the new contender.

media

News coverage

From time to time it is instructive to examine and reevaluate that medium which over the past fifty years or so has been quite instrumental in directing our lives for better or worse.

My comments will be restricted to the very specific area of news coverage on television for it is here where we are influenced, in large degree, as to who we are as Americans and who "they" are i.e., those in the international community.

In years past, news and news reporters presented to us relatively pure (at least as untainted as possible, given the human condition) reportage of those events occurring around us be it local, national or international. In other words, they were the conduit through which we were informed of those events, large or small, which had consequences to us as citizens. Of course, even as far back as early television there were "personalities" who were outstanding in their field and those individuals, because of their persona, drew us to them as avid followers of the events of the day.

What then has changed in the last fifty years in terms of the reporting of news on television? Understanding that vision through the rear mirror is always clearer and more forgiving than criticism of the current state of news reporting on television, here are some observations of both the current crop of reporters and the "stage" upon which they perform.

With the proliferation of sources of television news, we have been inundated with excessive reporting of any given event. The end result is constant repeating of the same news stories over and over again. After a period of time we are not sure if it is the same event about which we are hearing or just another repeat. My solution is to downsize the amount and frequency of news reporting. The result will be less redundancy and a more concise presentation given on a more meaningful, if less often, basis.

News presentations have become so competitive that I no longer consider them merely factual presentations of news, rather a bizarre and outlandish "show" with all of those gimmicks accompanying such Las Vegas type theatrical shows with all of the visual bells and whistles to make them competitive with the other "shows". Good old fashion news reporting has now become injected with a show business embellishment of the news which now becomes the center of attraction rather than a more serious exploration of news and issues. This of course results in news presenters interested more in presenting themselves as the center of attraction rather than the news.

A second and as disturbing element of today's "news shows" is a natural byproduct of this saturation of news on a twenty four hour seven day a week basis show business format resulting in the proliferation of "news bimbos" who, and I obviously exclude those few serous reporters of news, are more interested in how they look in their "part" of the show. The primary prerequisite for these positions seems to be whether or not the applicants have "star value" first as aspiring actresses rather than what their credentials are as professional reporters of the news.

Finally, an observation concerning the relationship between government and the news media is in order. For "we the people" to be appropriately informed as to the performance of our government, we must have an adversarial relationship between the government and the media. Today, the current connection is questionable. I am not so naïve as to understand that for the media to have "access" to governmental personages they require a "working" relationship. On the other hand, the media must not (as they are becoming) part of a social circle with those same governmental personages. The media, I believe, is becoming part of the "elite club" where they share social engagements with government officials. As curmudgeon like as I may appear, I think it is a fair assessment of the developing (if not already developed) partnership emerging between "our" media and the government. We must INSIST that the media play its rightful role as objective observer and reporter of events both national and international.

In sum, I am not attempting to roll back the clock to "the good old days". My suggestion is to downsize the excessive coverage of news and instead of the enormous "industry" which it has become, put it into a smaller and more manageable and productive space where NEWS is the subject, not the intensive and outlandish competition between the "stars" in an overblown industry.

government
Complex interplay

It is a complex web indeed that we weave. Blame plays an integral part in the complex interplay between government, media and the governed.

It is the government, in conjunction with large corporations which define not only how we live our lives, but those defined paths which are open to us in terms of lifestyle. We willingly, and maybe in some cases unwillingly play the “game”.

When things are running smoothly, there are no complaints from either side and all profit from the game. However, there is an ever present fly in the ointment. When the “game” becomes dysfunctional due to the strategy set down by government and big business, BLAME surfaces.

The current gas crisis is a point worth exploring. We have been encouraged by our leaders both in government and big business to pursue a certain lifestyle of excess materialism. This of course includes unlimited use of a precious source of a limited resource. i.e., oil. The inevitable follows. Too much demand for a limited supply and where does the blame fall? Of course, on the backs of the citizens for not taking a more conservative approach to their life style which government and big business encouraged. Of course in the run up to the crisis, THEY take credit for the improved lifestyle, but when "the game" begins to crumble, it is WE who have to make serious adjustments to our lifestyles which they were instrumental in creating. CREDIT to government and big business for an affluent and excessive lifestyle until it becomes dysfunctional and BLAME to the general citizenry who are playing the game which THEY created when the game becomes dysfunctional.

On another level, BLAME becomes an aspect of cannibalism in the government itself. "Power corrupts and absolute power corrupts absolutely" Words to that effect have been stated historically. The current administration has been in COMPLETE control for a number of years and their power has grown exponentially. However, the pendulum can only swing in one direction until the momentum determines that it changes direction. The media which, as always, fall in line like sheep and pay homage to the government in power due in part to the "perks" of participating in the game are in fact vultures that are waiting for the power to shift so they can participate in the feeding frenzy. At the appropriate time when they see the shifting of power, they and the opponents of the regime in power close in for the kill and the feeding frenzy begins. They wait in turn for access to the carcass as vultures wait for the lion to have his fill. There are no allies in government and media, only temporary alliances until the winds shift. That is the nature of power.

government

The threat

The threat, both potential and real, to the United States would appear to be in the east. My assumption is that in fact the conflicts in that area will be resolved short of outright war in the entire area based on two presumptions.

First, ten years or less from now oil will not be an issue since alternative forms of energy will emerge to replace this valuable liquid and second, we cannot and will not sustain an open ended conflict in the area. The resolution will come as a result of a tedious negotiating process and more realistic stances which will be taken by both sides. Once the oil factor is removed from the equation, our "interest" in the area will drop precipitously.

Of a much more serious and long term threat to the United States is the developing situation in the area south of us in our own hemisphere. There is currently turmoil and unrest in several areas south of the border. In recent years democratic elections have put into office freely elected officials who have a distinct anti-United States flavor. Ironically, Cuba, our "arch enemy" in the area is right in the middle of this new and growing alliance in the area. In fact, our popularity rating world wide is at the lowest ebb in the history of the United States. Whether or not the administration notices or even cares about the worldwide perception is inconsequential. The fact is that the rest of the world in general has lost faith in our version of that dream of freedom and democracy based on the actions of the current administration. That dream however is still alive in the eyes of other nations. Our problem is that this particular administration has lost sight of its own dreams and the current administration has "stolen" that precious commodity and replaced it with our own form of a creeping dictatorship.

The position into which we have placed ourselves is a policy of backing "democratic" regimes throughout the world with the caveat that they must be "our" kind of democracies. The current hard line policy of our current administration has alienated many of our neighbors. The principal that you are either for us or you are the enemy has backed us into a corner. Our current neighbors who are resisting this hard line today have alternatives to accepting our simplistic dictum of either being for us or against us. Ironically, it is our former adversary "red" China, that totalitarian state which is repositioning itself as the rising leader of the newly emerging democratic states especially in South America. We are in fact losing control of many nations in our own back yard! What we have failed to recognize is that the theory of totalitarian China is in fact changing before our very eyes. The totalitarian government in China is in fact being co-opted by the growing entrepreneurial Chinese free enterprise sector. In fact, the Chinese government, recognizing the benefits of an "open" society is not only reluctantly accepting the new freedom in China, but is in fact participating in the changing order in the country.

Our outdated foreign policy is misreading the face of the new China and we will pay dearly unless we install new leadership in our country which recognizes this fact and makes drastic changes in our foreign policy.

government
The Dubaiport

What is the public hue and cry over the Dubaiport issue? To be as objective as possible, I will say up front that I am neither for nor against the concept. The issue I believe is whether you are a proponent of nationalism or internationalism. The "Dubaiport" issue is merely the tip of the iceberg of a critical moment in the history of modern civilization!

Had this issue not have been exposed to the light of public scrutiny this would have been merely one of those "secret" arrangements made between consenting countries. International business deals have always existed. What has made this situation unique is that for the first time, nationalism and internationalism have come head to head in a unique manner.

I have said in a previous article that nationalism may be at the root of many of the international crises. Having a "they" as an adversary has allowed many countries the option of creating a devil which they must defeat at all costs. This has been true throughout history where there has always been a hierarchy of power amongst nations. If this constant presence of conflict has its roots in nationalism and if in today's world this is an option which is unacceptable, what then is the alternative?

Internationalism or a "one world order" seems to be the obvious choice. If in fact this is the case, how might the opponents of the one world order respond?

The first and most obvious question is whether or not an international power which cuts across national borders is in fact workable. In other words are all nations amenable to ceding their national integrity and decision making to a "world" government? This would be most critical to those countries currently in positions of power. A second and possibly even stickier problem is how a nation which is currently in a preeminent power position will REDUCE its economic and military power position without drastic ramifications within its own borders.

To date in a world of nationalism there has been a vertical division dividing "us" from "them". The international consolidation of power would create a horizontal division of power wherein all power would reside in some form of an international body which would control all citizens of the world. Herein lies the current contradiction of the Dubai ports proposal. At its core, the current issue of perception is as important as the actual facts on the ground.

For the past several years, we have been "exporting" our jobs. It began with the exporting of basic level jobs and has now expanded to the exporting of management positions. As expertly as the government and big business has tried to manipulate public perception of the process the American public has finally caught on to the process of big business, in the name of profit for the corporation is exporting OUR jobs at OUR expense.

The American citizen is quite forgiving of its government and will bend over backwards to support public policy UNTIL it perceives that it is being "used" by its big business and government representatives to line their pockets while at the same time "evening out" the lifestyle of American citizens with those foreign citizens to whom the jobs are being exported.

At this very moment when the American worker feels insecure because of this movement of outsourcing, along comes "Dubaiport" and the perception, or possibly reality that our government is sacrificing OUR national interests to some vague global entity which includes OUR government AND our large corporations who are now becoming servants to this larger entity at the expense of its own citizens.

The jury is still out as to the outcome of this sea change. It is possible that the American citizens will accept the new direction and fall in line to become part of an international brotherhood of workers OR rampant nationalism might win the day and our politicians might be taken to task and accept the responsibility of righting the ship or suffer the consequences which may indeed be dire.

government
Out of control

Day by day government is getting more and more out of control. My concern is that as it grows, larger portions of our hard earned money are being extracted from our pay checks. The harder we work the less take home pay we realize.

In our representative form of government, it is those leaders whom we vote into office that supposedly represent our interests. This may have been the case years ago when they were people who truly represented us.

In recent years, what has evolved is a separate segment of “royalty” which only incidentally represents us. In fact unlike in past times when our legislators served their constituency with minimal reimbursement, truly represented us then left to construct their futures in the private sector, over the past few decades a “package” has been developed whereby their term in office is now a lucrative career which guarantees them very beneficial retirement packages which far outweigh those packages which we ordinary citizens could ever approximate.

The motivation is no longer to serve a period as our representatives; rather it has become their life time jobs! Simply stated, they represent us minimally but their main concern is growing their personal financial careers. What we must demand is that they be rewarded modestly, that is a paycheck and benefits comparable to ours and they must participate in the same programs that ordinary citizens participate. Their motivation and reward should be to serve a term and to serve the public then leave! Those elected officials whom we currently have as our representatives are a separate breed of individuals. Individuals, may I say who are in office mainly for their own self interest and incidentally, and only incidentally for the good of the citizens whom they serve.

They are quite aware of the pent up outrage out here in "the private sector" and they have developed various strategies to counter this growing public indignation. "Term limits" is the current sleight of hand being used. It is suggested that if we limit the term in office, we will limit the "influence" wielded by these legislators.

The length of term in office is not the problem since they can realize all of those long term benefits during a short term in office. The problem is "the package" which they have created for themselves.

What is needed is to CHANGE the package so as not to give them the incentive to stay in office! It is not far from the truth to suggest that whatever their status prior to serving the public, when they leave office, the vast majority of our representatives are millionaires. Greed I would suggest is the current motivation of our legislators.

One of the arguments for the current package suggests that if we don't pay our representatives adequately we will not have in office TOP people to represent our interests. Rubbish I say! You cannot BUY excellent legislators. What is needed is commitment to the common good. The current motivation of wealth which we are offering our legislators merely draws upon those greedy individuals whose prime interest is their own self interest. An adequate remuneration during their term in office without the perks currently being offered will bring out the best in our citizen legislators. Let those who believe that they require the EXTRAS to be good legislators find jobs in the private sector where they can realize their dreams, or not.

In my personal finances, it is I who determine the health or lack thereof regarding my personal portfolio and retirement package. It is therefore in my self-interest to ensure the healthiest position for both me and my family..

If our representatives have the same retirement, health insurance and other benefits as we, I can assure you that their decisions for spending the public money which will in effect be theirs will differ substantially from the current situation where they are spending public money and not suffering the same consequences as other citizens since they currently are in fact "outside" the system.

government

The third party

Time for the third party is upon us. There is still time between now and the next presidential election. Those pundits who say that a third party candidate cannot realistically expect to successfully compete with the two major powers because of the enormous cost of campaigning and the entrenched bureaucracy of the current two party system have very strong arguments indeed. The dilemma is that the current system is becoming dysfunctional in that it is not representing those citizens to whom it should be obligated.

The first obstacle which must be overcome is the nature of the current representatives of the citizens. Over the years the parameters defining who should be our representatives has changed. Slowly but inevitably the "perks" of office have increased to the point whereby it has BECOME the reason for new representatives to enter the system. In early America those who were elected were not rewarded to the point where they would stay in office. Control of the public coffers and influence by big business has become too large an incentive for our representatives to ignore.

A new royalty has emerged, a royalty which owes its allegiance to both outside and inside interests i.e., big business interests and "perks" which have been built into the very system they control. Lip service is what the ordinary citizens are receiving. A widening chasm is emerging whereby a small minority of vested government EMPLOYEES, large business interests and wealthy citizens who have profited from the new royalty. Left out of this system is the growing population of ordinary citizens who have put their future and well being in the hands of the new royalty.

Unfortunately, the new leadership has not to date been able to recognize this growing distance between themselves and the general population.

Two admonitions will be issued to this new royalty. First, there is an undocumented and unwritten guideline to which our representatives must adhere; that is, the spread of wealth and well being must filter down to the least representative citizens of a nation. Although there is no written formula for this "equality" and in fact those with "more" will always have a larger portion of the pie, if the vast majority of citizens who are at the lower end of the spectrum reach a point where participation in the system becomes more of a burden than a reward, the nation will be at the edge of a revolution. It is incumbent upon those who "have" to avoid the temptation of having "all".

Secondly, history has shown us that societies do in fact disintegrate and in many cases the fall of society comes from within rather than from invasion from a foreign enemy.

The motivation for our current leaders does not reward them for maintaining this balance between the many working citizens and the clique of leaders both in and out of government. The current two party system of Democrats and Republicans have lost sight of those whom they are supposed to represent and as has been said by a former governor who said that "there is not a dime's difference between the parties". However difficult the task, short of the two party system reforming itself, a third party must emerge which is motivated by truly playing its role in a representative democracy and avoiding the self aggrandizement of the current system. In short, what is needed is a different type of representative with different motivations. If this party does not emerge, I fear that the current two party system is not motivated and prepared to halt the growing chasm between royalty and the common citizen. Continued disregard for the current citizen may indeed lead to truly dire consequences.

government
Liberal or conservative

Am I a Liberal or Conservative? Am I a Democrat or Republican? Twenty years ago the answer would have been quite a bit simpler. The world and our perceptions today have not only become quite a bit more complex, but definitions have become quite a bit murkier.

I am a firm believer in equality between the sexes, but I am adamantly against single motherhood and the "single mom" accepted expression of the day.

I am for protecting United States markets against outside and unfair trading practices but as Thomas L. Friedman in his new book "The World is Flat", suggests, markets are becoming international at an exponential pace and I understand and accept this new direction in the 21st century.

I am, as most Americans are, firmly against international terrorism and will defend our position against this new kind of war. On the other hand I am adamantly against our perfidious intrusion into Iraq and believe we are painting ourselves into an unacceptable corner, the escape from which will be next to impossible without serious consequences.

I am for a woman's choice concerning the abortion issue but am steadfastly against abortion

I have always been in the corner of the Civil Rights Movement and equality before the law for all citizens but am abhorred by the overuse of the "race card" as a tool to make the field "uneven".

I am in favor of giving a more equitable share of our nations wealth to the poorest members of our society for it is how they are treated which will eventually define who we are as a nation. At the same time I am quite distressed with the current welfare state which encourages many of our citizens to take advantage of the public coffers.

Readers of this article will probably assume that I am quite confused and unable to take a clear stance on a given issue and he or she is probably correct for the most part. To respond to the "muddled" state of my positions on these issues I simply ask two probing questions for evaluation of my "muddled" positions concerning these issues.

1. Are most Americans in this same quandary?

2. Have many of the issues over the last twenty years become co-mingled and immersed in muddy waters by our political leaders thus not permitting us the ability to take clear positions on many of the issues and affording THEM quite a bit of "wiggle" room in which they can swim without getting caught?

Am I overly cynical? I leave it to the reader to decide.

government

Social security system

Let us explore the current Social Security system. I believe it is safe to assume that all agree that there has to be change. The simple fact, and that may be oversimplification given the complexity of the issue, is that if we are to believe what we are told that in coming years there will be too many recipients for the number of working people supporting the system, that system as we know it must be changed. The words which are critical to the solution are "gradualism" and "transition".

Let us attempt at constructing the framework for a new Social Security system understanding that whatever the formula, some people will disagree due to the various cut off points in the new structure and how these cutoff points will affect them.

Step 1: All citizens who are eligible for Social Security from age 55 and older will collect full Social Security and continue to pay their FICA obligation.

Step 2: Citizens from 50 years of age to 55 years of age will collect 85% of their Social Security benefits upon retirement and they will contribute a percentage less than they now contribute to FICA (percentage to be determined) It will be their responsibility to invest the difference between the lower FICA contribution and the full FICA contribution for which they were responsible into a 401B savings program.

Step 3: All Citizens up to 50 years of age will collect 80% of Social Security benefits upon retirement and they will contribute a percentage less than they now contribute to FICA (again percentage to be determined) and as in Step 2 above it will be their responsibility to invest the difference between the lower FICA contribution and the full FICA contribution for which they were responsible into a 401B savings program.

Step 4: Fica deductions will change from the current $90,000.00 to $140,000.00.

I believe the above formula for a changed Social Security System will be a good guideline for a structure which will take us into the foreseeable future. Of course with a program which affects so many of our citizens we must remember that the "devil is in the detail" and some of the aspects of the program will have to be scrutinized and resolved by our leaders such as

1. Should all citizens who have over a certain dollar figure of unearned income upon retirement be eligible for the program?

2. Should it be mandatory for all of those savings in the 401B programs have some sort of oversight to ensure that the individual investors don't squander "their savings?"

3. Should all citizens contribute to the FICA account regardless of their earnings?

Lastly, the Social Security program and any outside financial savings plans will not be commingled. The current Social Security System with the above alterations must be retained as the social program for which it was instituted.

It is hoped that this article will act as a mechanism to open up a long overdue and serious discussion of the issue which affects us.

government

Term limits

Term limits has been on the table for a number of years. The assumption is that the longer an elected official remains in office the more he becomes part of the "problem" in the system.

To buttress this argument, one of our own politicians who ran for state office on the strength of his argument that he would remain in his elected position for the designated term as per his contract then return to the "dreaded private sector" and go on with his life as a private citizen.

Well, guess what? As he reached the end of his term in office, he found that he was doing so much "good" for his constituents that it became imperative that he extend his stay in office beyond the designated term. He therefore ran for reelection and was returned to office and remains there today. The truth, I propose, is that once he got a taste of "the benefits" of the office beyond a paycheck, he was placed in a position where it became "an offer he couldn't refuse". We are now at what I consider the crux of the problem.

The office has become so attractive as a career with many and varied "freebies" above and beyond the salary of the office that it becomes next to impossible for our representatives to leave office and replace that lucrative package they have as our representatives and their "no heavy lifting" jobs.

The true problem I suggest is not the term limits of the position because the true culprit is not the length of term in office, but the structure of the positions of our elected officials. Their "program" has become so lucrative, a program which has evolved over the years, that "our" representatives will fight like tomcats not only to remain in office with the generous salary which we pay them, but for the "benefit package" they gratefully accept which goes far beyond the salary and which many of those of us in the private sector would eagerly accept. What must take place is a total revamping of the system so that our representatives are "rewarded" for leaving office i.e., offering them a living wage while in office doing the public good while eliminating the extra benefits which motivate them to stay in office. They must be motivated to return to the private sector!

I realize that the devil is in the detail and that the office has become so attractive and lucrative to those in office that "restructuring" the benefit package to the benefit of the citizens and not for the representatives may well be impossible since it is they who structure the package.

An example is in order in my personal life. We live in a condominium complex. The elected board which determines the management of the condominium consists of non paid members who are also condominium owners. Since they are not paid, it behooves them to keep costs down while at the same time maintaining the integrity of the building. It is in their interest to efficiently and judiciously manage the building since the required money to maintain the building comes out of their pockets also and we all play by the same rules!

Likewise with our state representatives, if they are in the same boat with us and suffer the same consequences, their performance will be truly representative of "us" since they will be part of "us" and suffer the same ups and downs resulting from their decision making.

Under the current system they have their own set of rules which although applying to all, allows them "loopholes" through their benefit packages to insulate them from much of the legislation which affects other citizens. In effect, they are outside the system. Due to the insulation as a result of their benefits program it assists them in making those "hard" decisions which affect the rest of us while minimally affecting them. In the end, it is always easier to make hard decisions to be imposed upon others while we insulate ourselves from many of the effects of such hard decision making.

Cover and page layout design by Samantha Wilder Oliver, Billerica, MA.

www.ingramcontent.com/pod-product-compliance
Ingram Content Group UK Ltd.
Pitfield, Milton Keynes, MK11 3LW, UK
UKHW041846190726
13854UKWH00002B/750

9 781425 102142